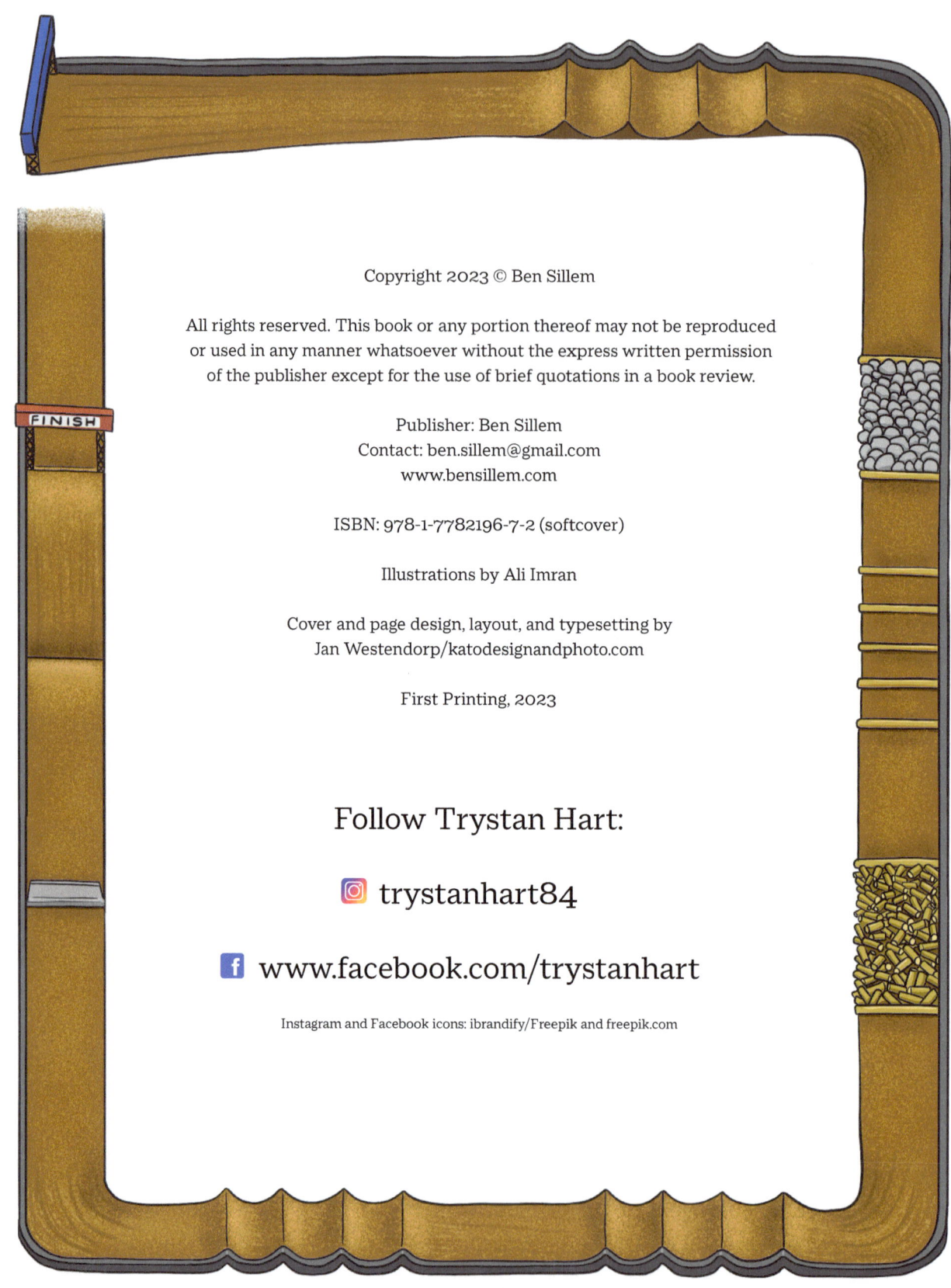

Copyright 2023 © Ben Sillem

All rights reserved. This book or any portion thereof may not be reproduced or used in any manner whatsoever without the express written permission of the publisher except for the use of brief quotations in a book review.

Publisher: Ben Sillem
Contact: ben.sillem@gmail.com
www.bensillem.com

ISBN: 978-1-7782196-7-2 (softcover)

Illustrations by Ali Imran

Cover and page design, layout, and typesetting by
Jan Westendorp/katodesignandphoto.com

First Printing, 2023

Follow Trystan Hart:

trystanhart84

www.facebook.com/trystanhart

Instagram and Facebook icons: ibrandify/Freepik and freepik.com

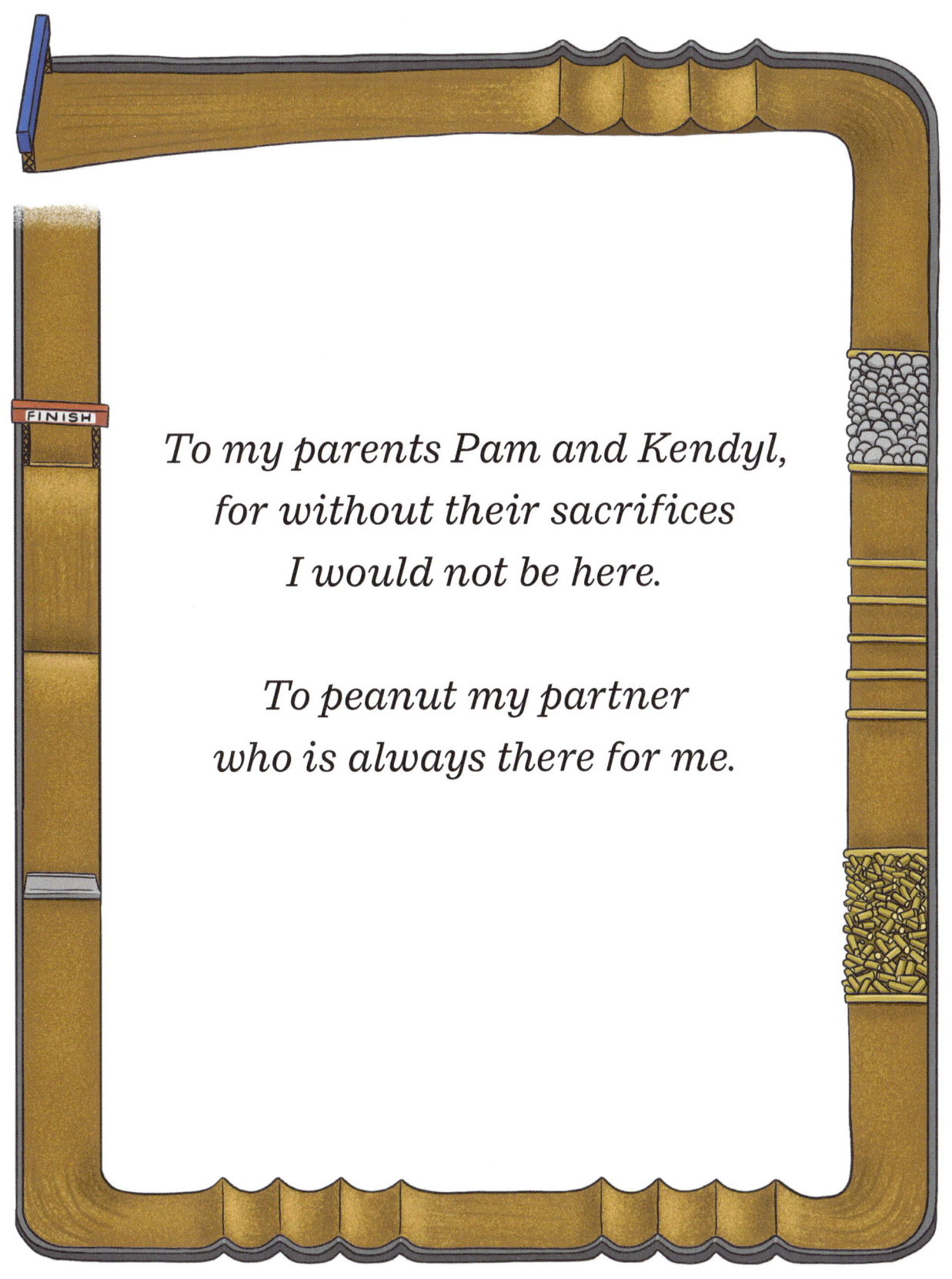

*To my parents Pam and Kendyl,
for without their sacrifices
I would not be here.*

*To peanut my partner
who is always there for me.*

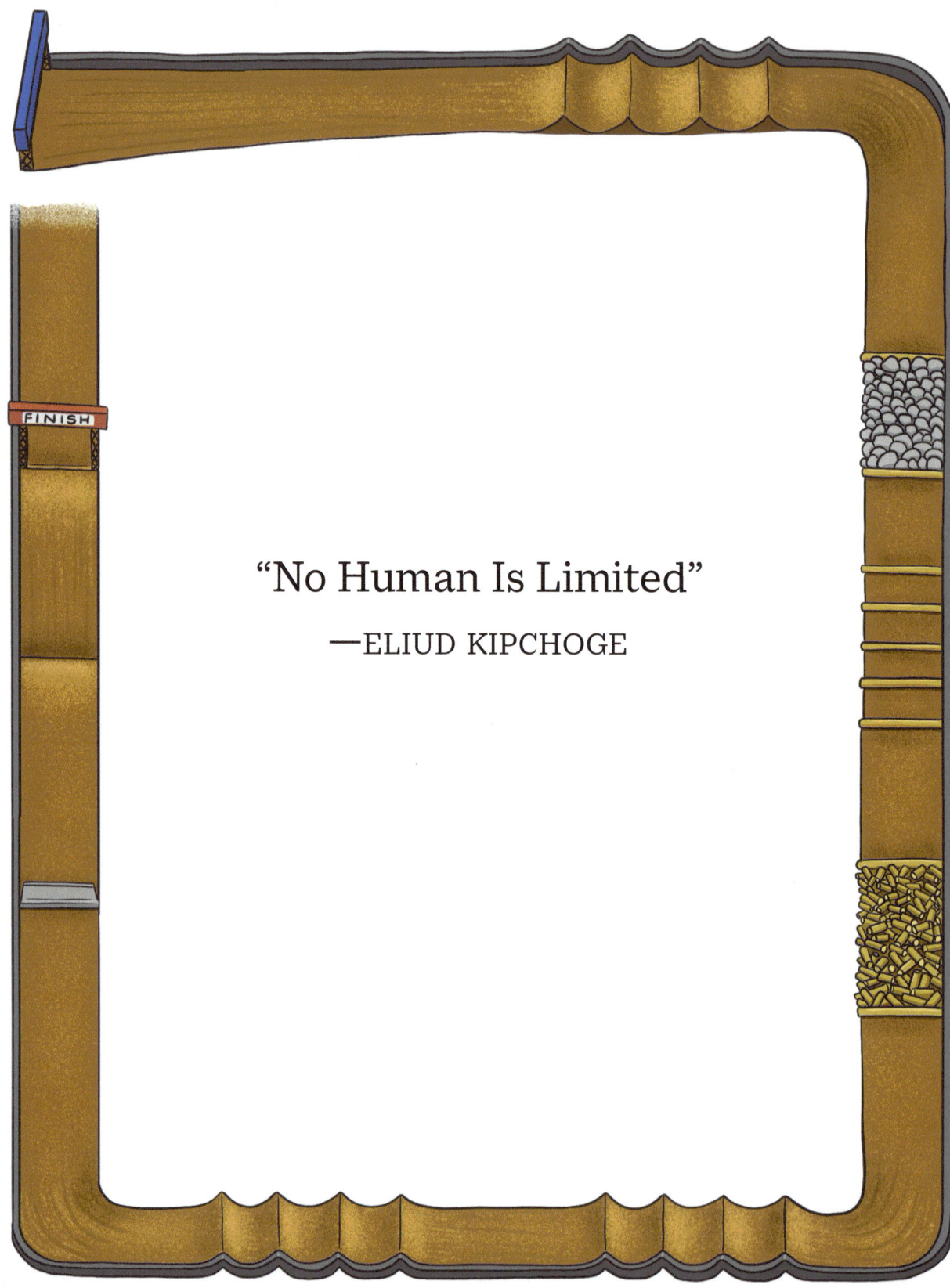

"No Human Is Limited"

—ELIUD KIPCHOGE

Since I was
a little tyke

All I wanted was
time on a dirt bike.

In my room I'd pretend to zoom

Long before I became one with my machine,

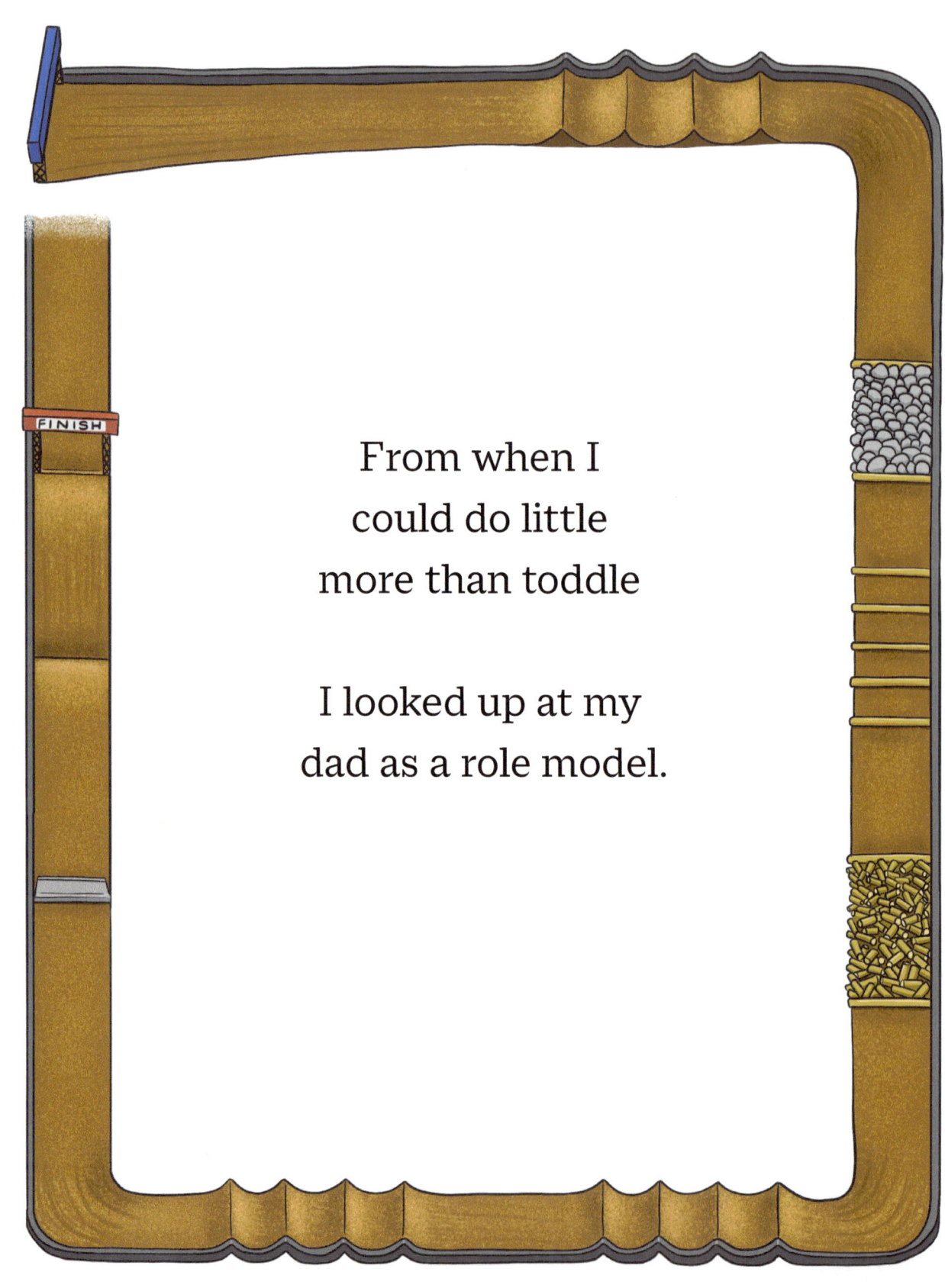

From when I could do little more than toddle

I looked up at my dad as a role model.

He taught me
how to ride

And in my bike
to take pride.

My brother, sisters, and even mom

Also got in on dirt bike fun.

Already on that backyard track

I wanted to be at the front of the pack.

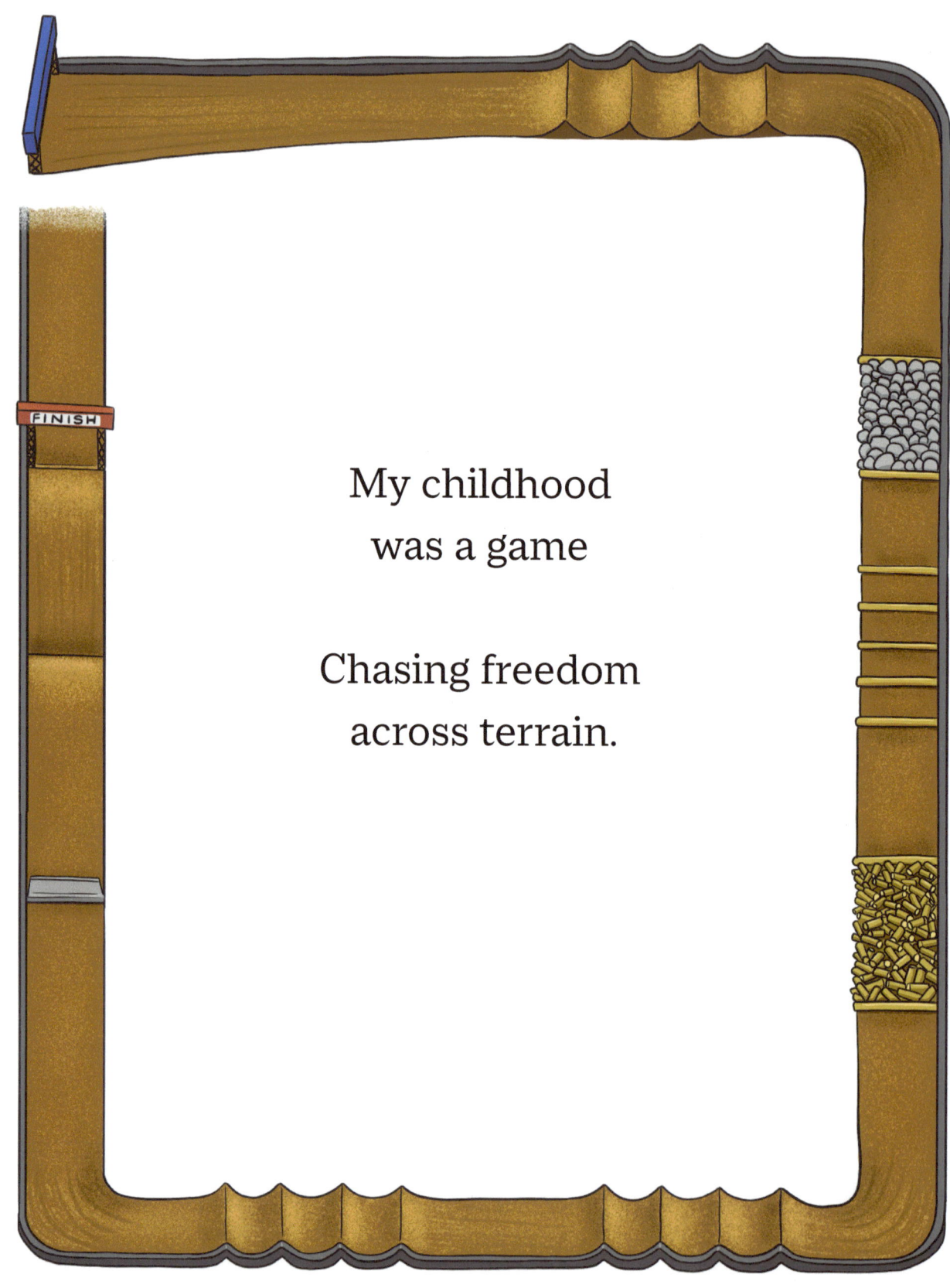

My childhood
was a game

Chasing freedom
across terrain.

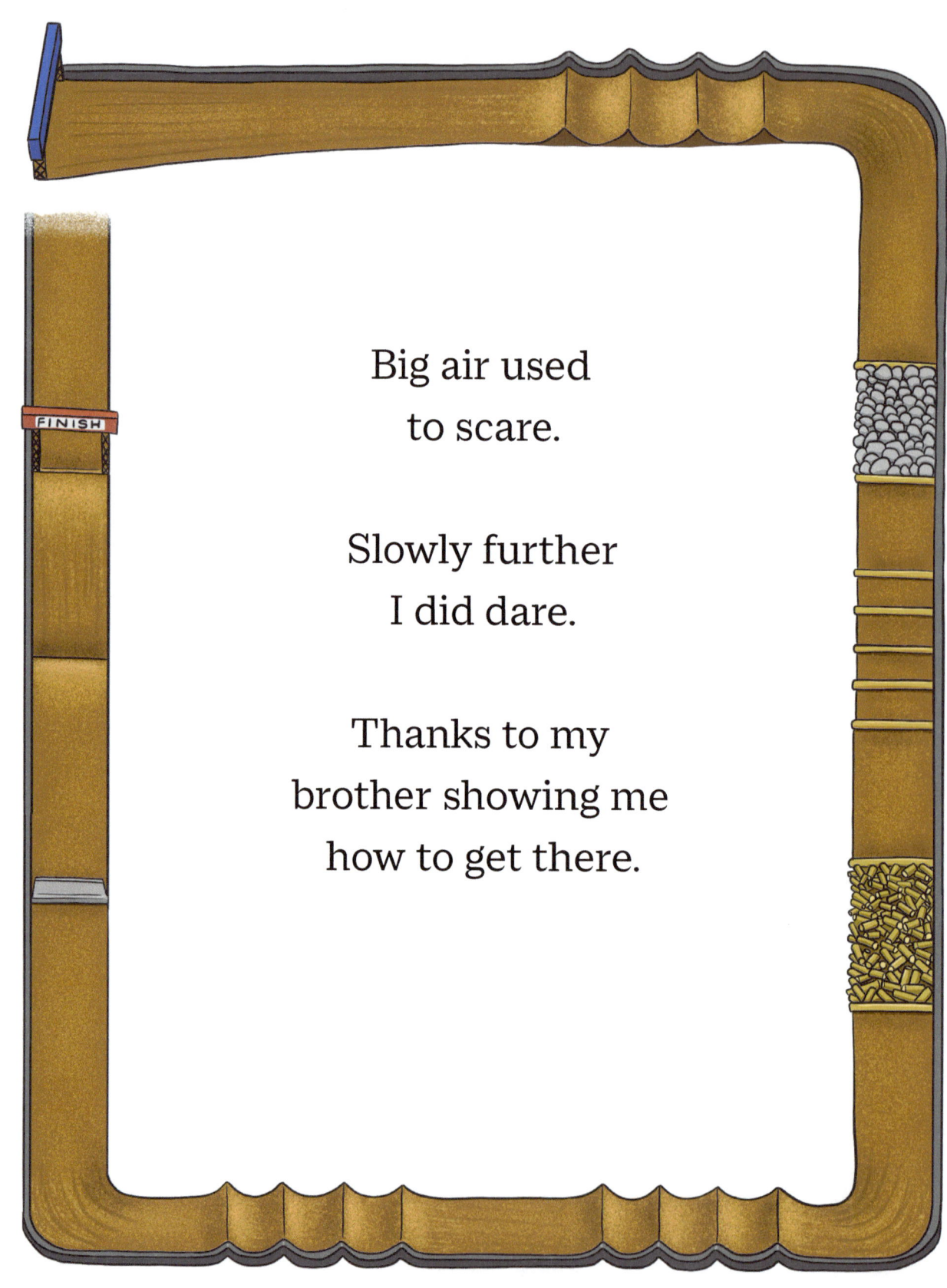

Big air used
to scare.

Slowly further
I did dare.

Thanks to my
brother showing me
how to get there.

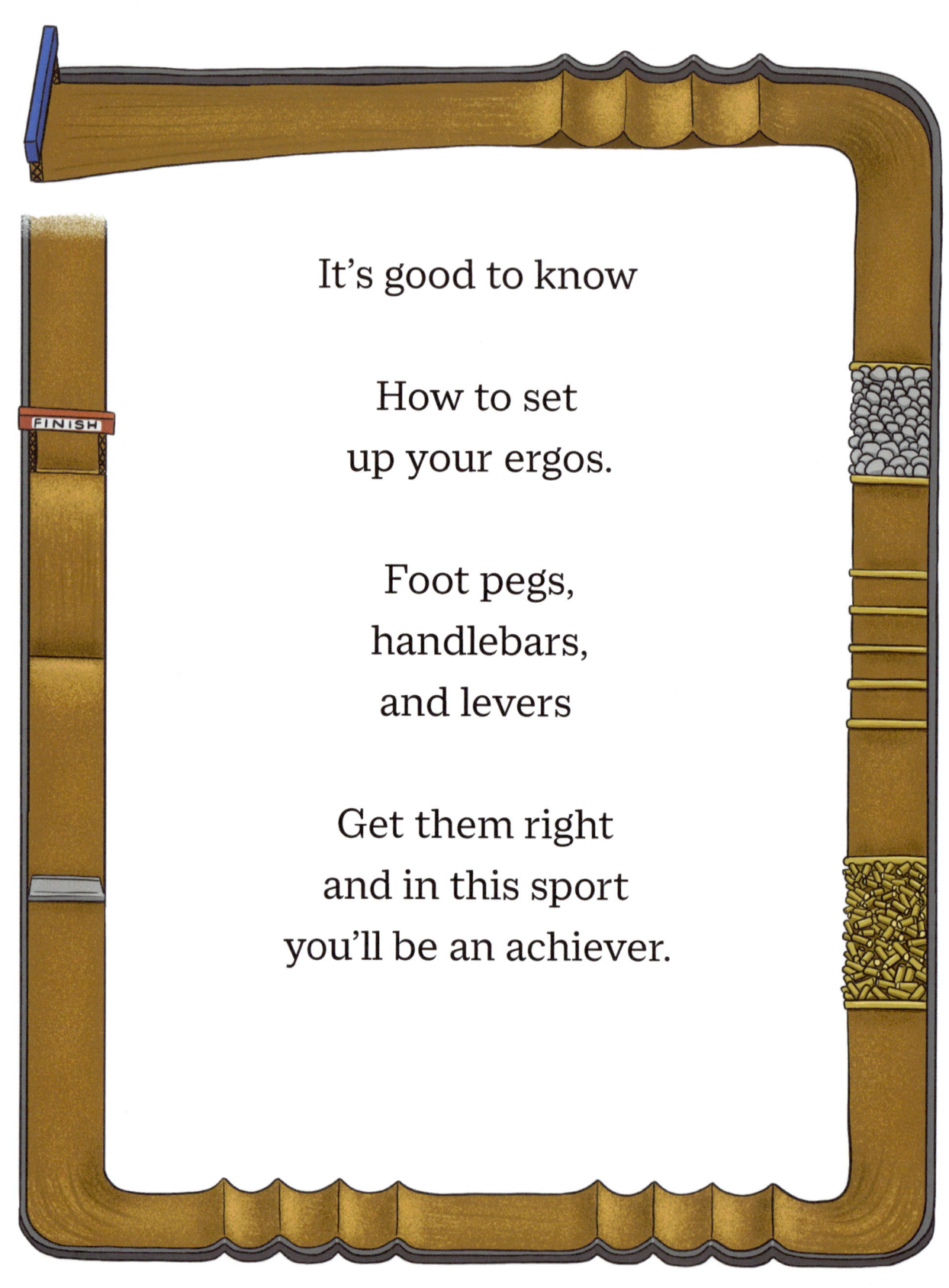

It's good to know

How to set
up your ergos.

Foot pegs,
handlebars,
and levers

Get them right
and in this sport
you'll be an achiever.

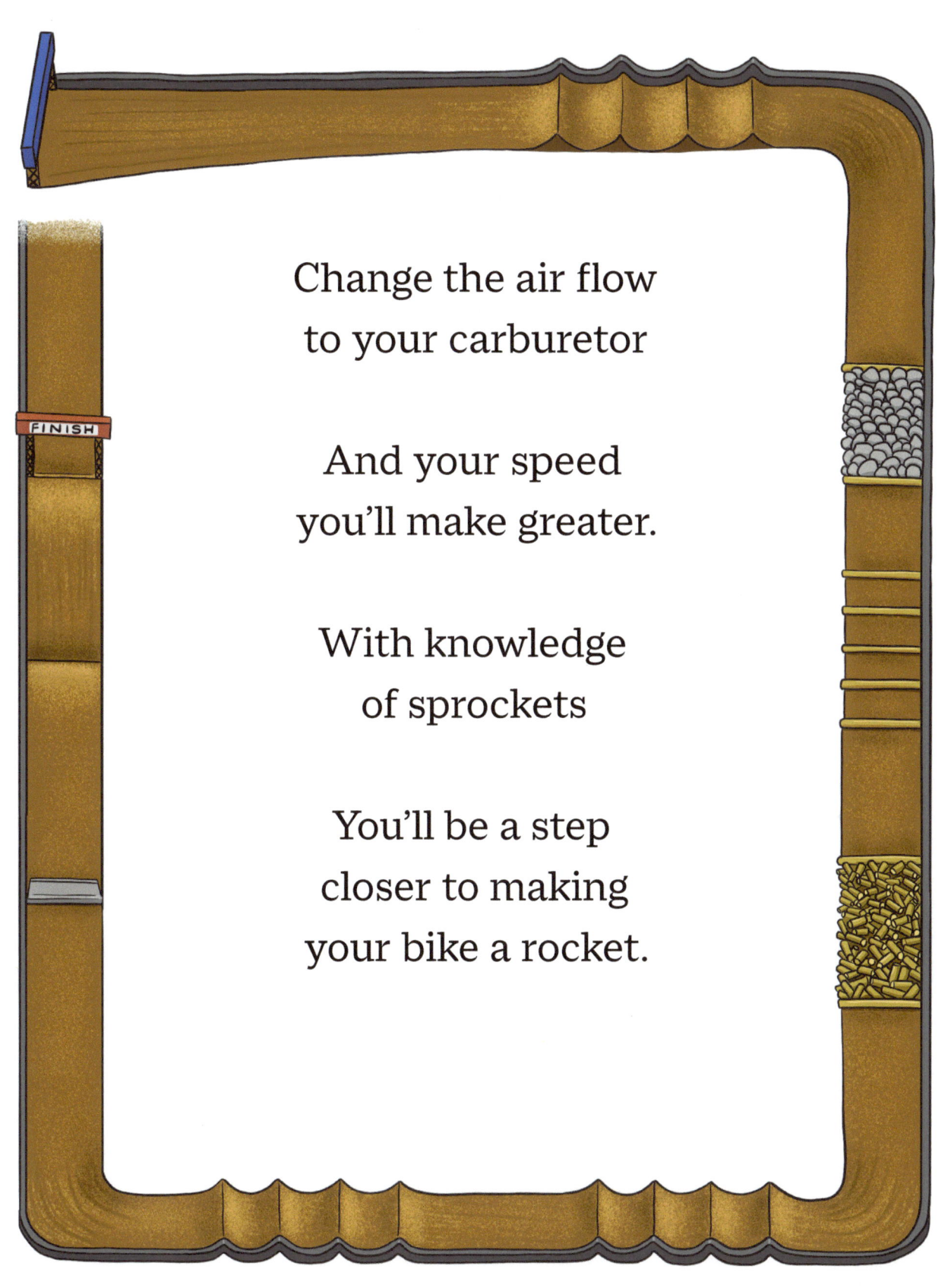

Change the air flow
to your carburetor

And your speed
you'll make greater.

With knowledge
of sprockets

You'll be a step
closer to making
your bike a rocket.

Before I head out

Of my bike's condition, I have no doubt.

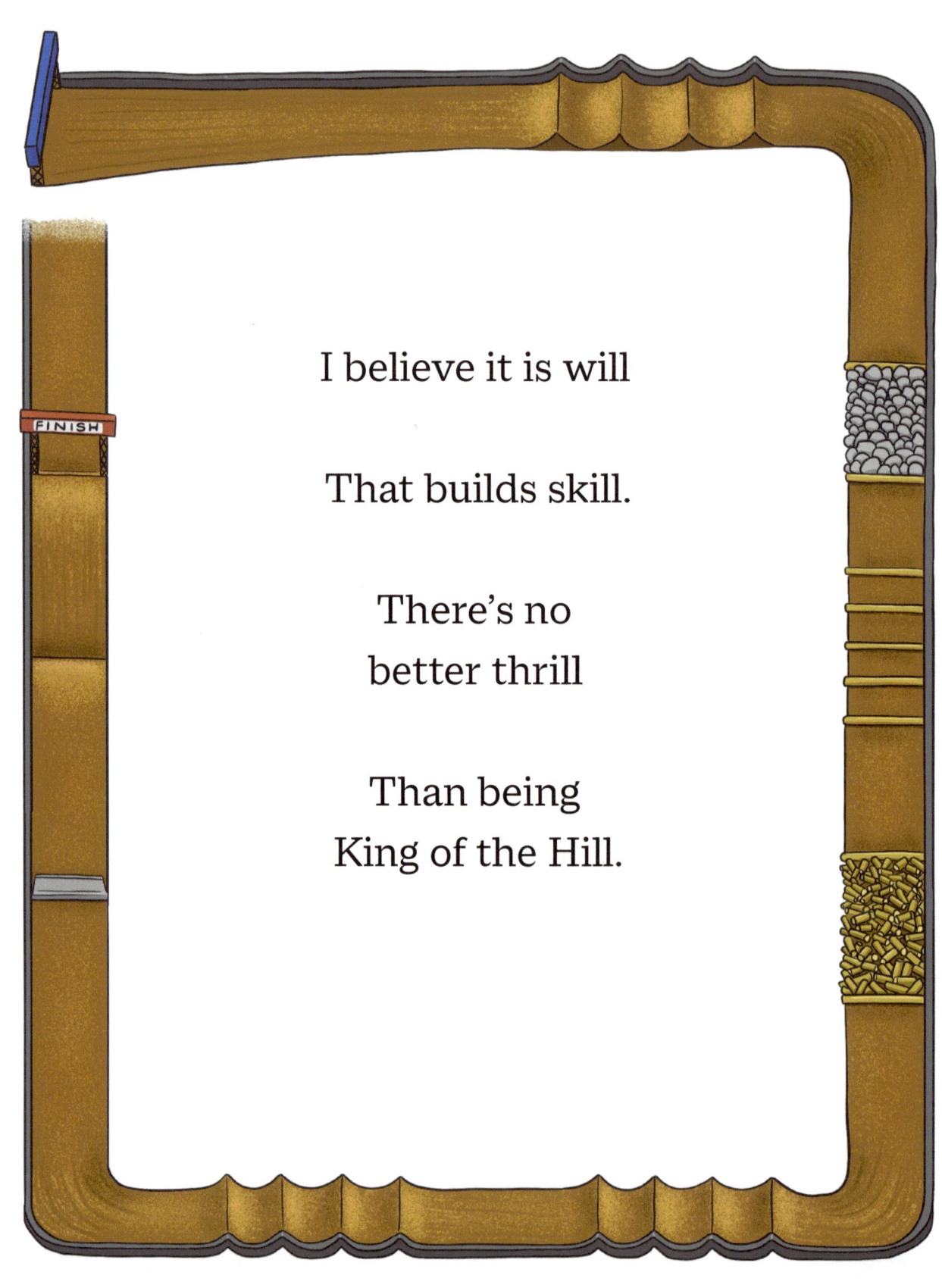

I believe it is will

That builds skill.

There's no
better thrill

Than being
King of the Hill.

Nature's rugged terrain

Seems designed to be a pain

Overcoming it is the core of this game.

Stay forward
in your seat

For unstable
terrain to meet.

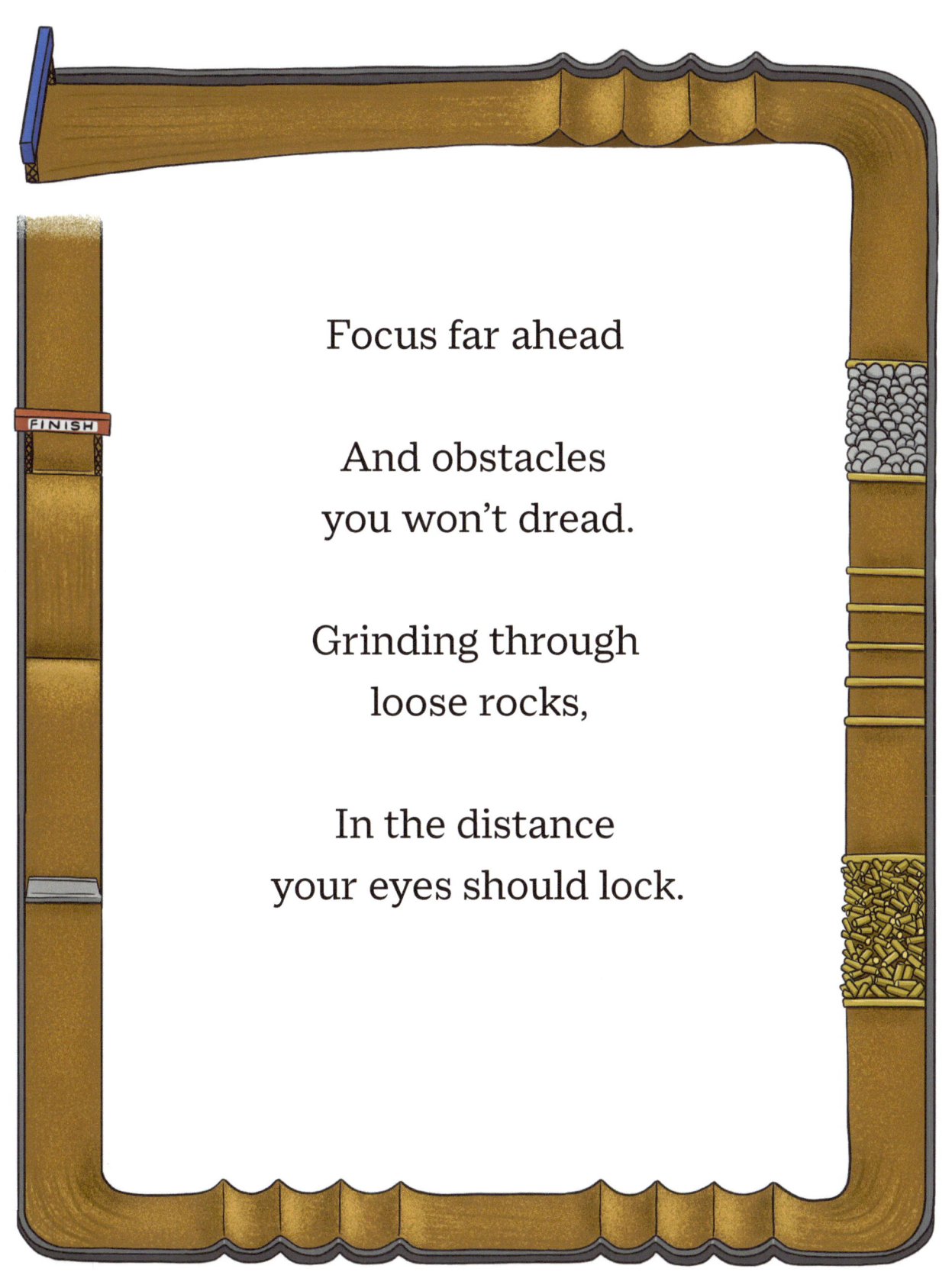

Focus far ahead

And obstacles
you won't dread.

Grinding through
loose rocks,

In the distance
your eyes should lock.

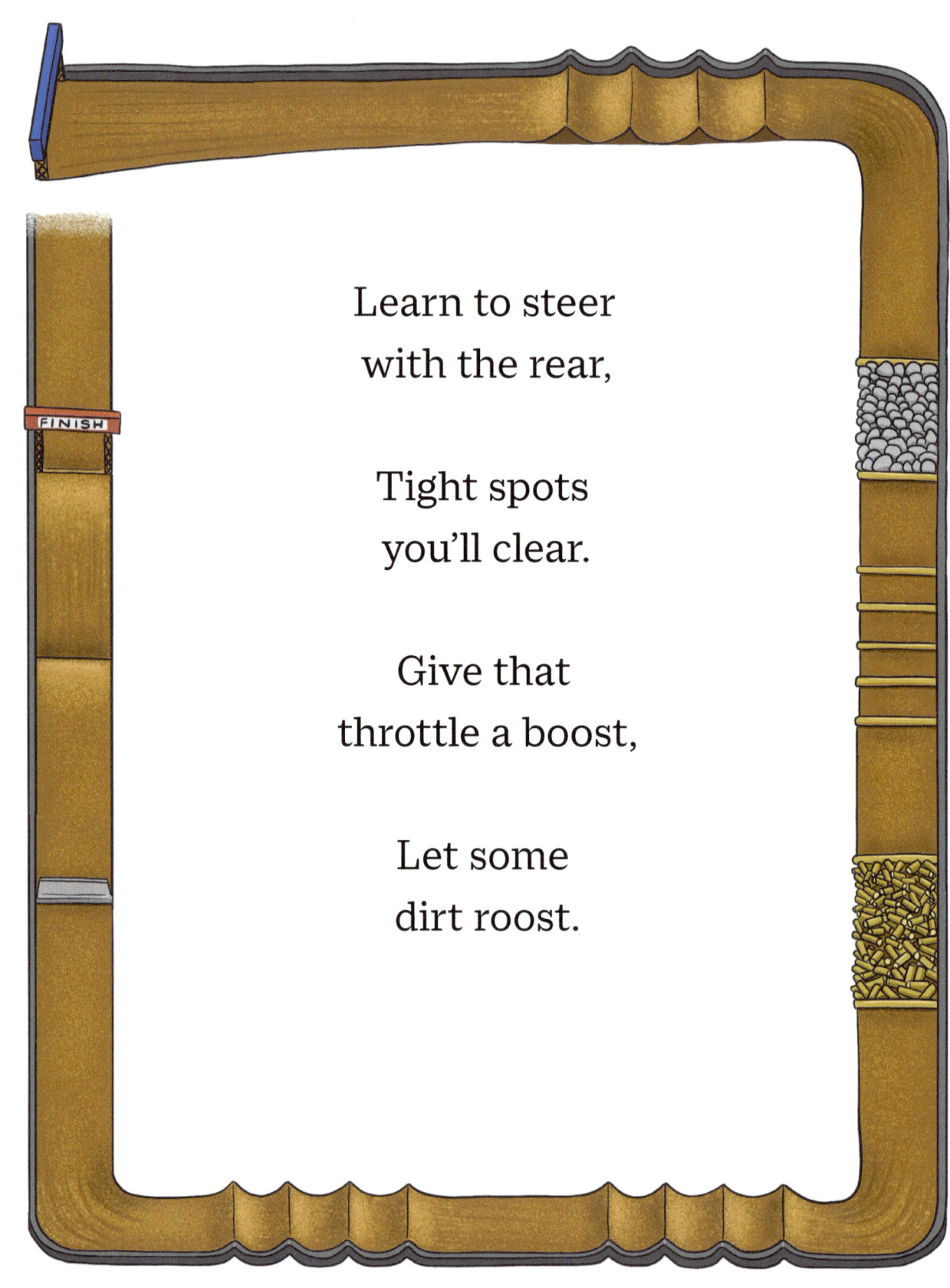

Learn to steer
with the rear,

Tight spots
you'll clear.

Give that
throttle a boost,

Let some
dirt roost.

To avoid
becoming bogged

Over top a beefy log,

Roll up to it with
front tire square,

And bounce front
fork with throttle to
get over there.

First or last

Enduro's
always a blast.

Though you
can reliably bet,

In this activity
you're going to sweat.

Dirt, hurt, and grime

All are part
of my good time.

Climbing over
big boulders

Takes a toll on
wrists and shoulders.

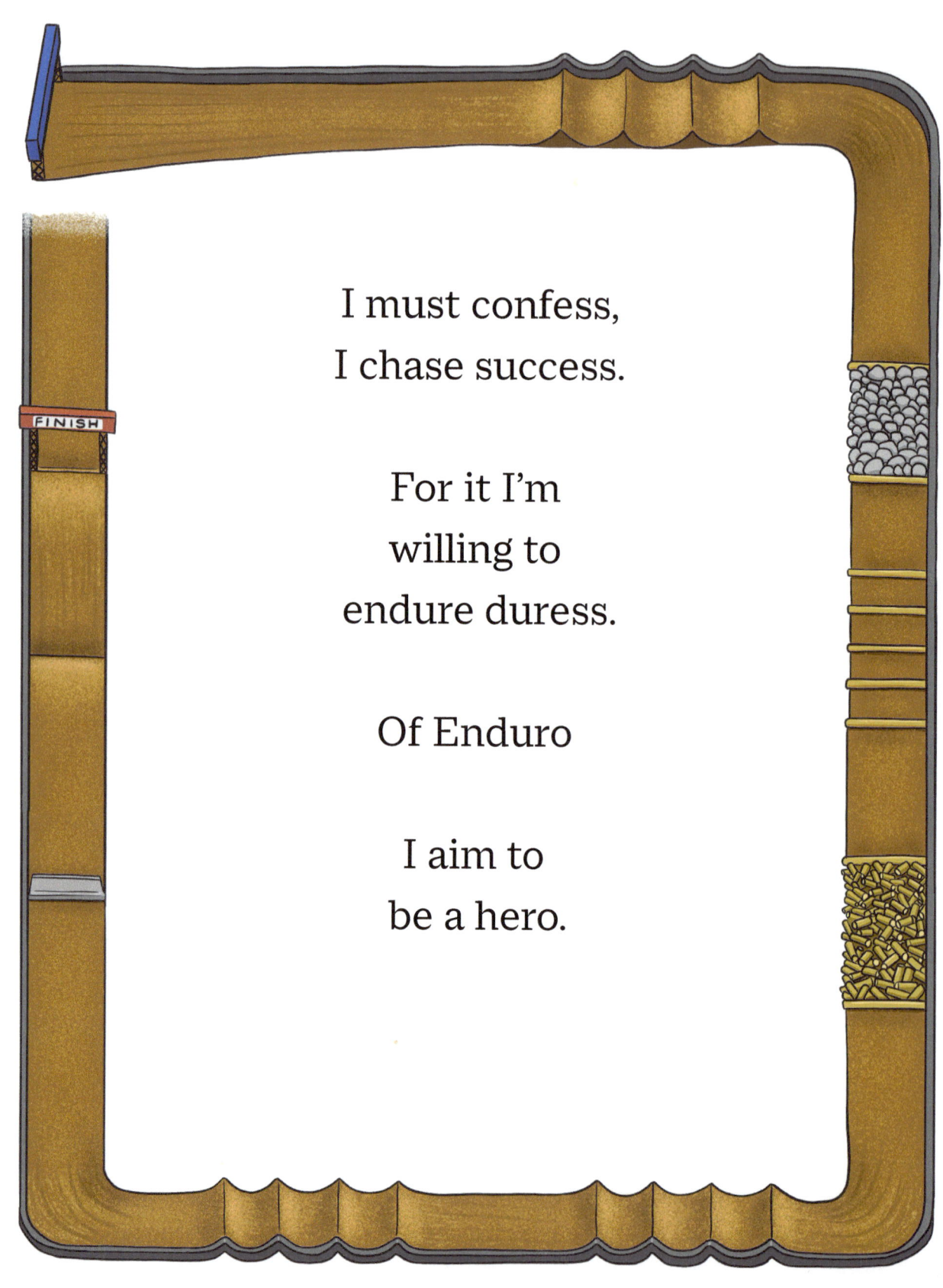

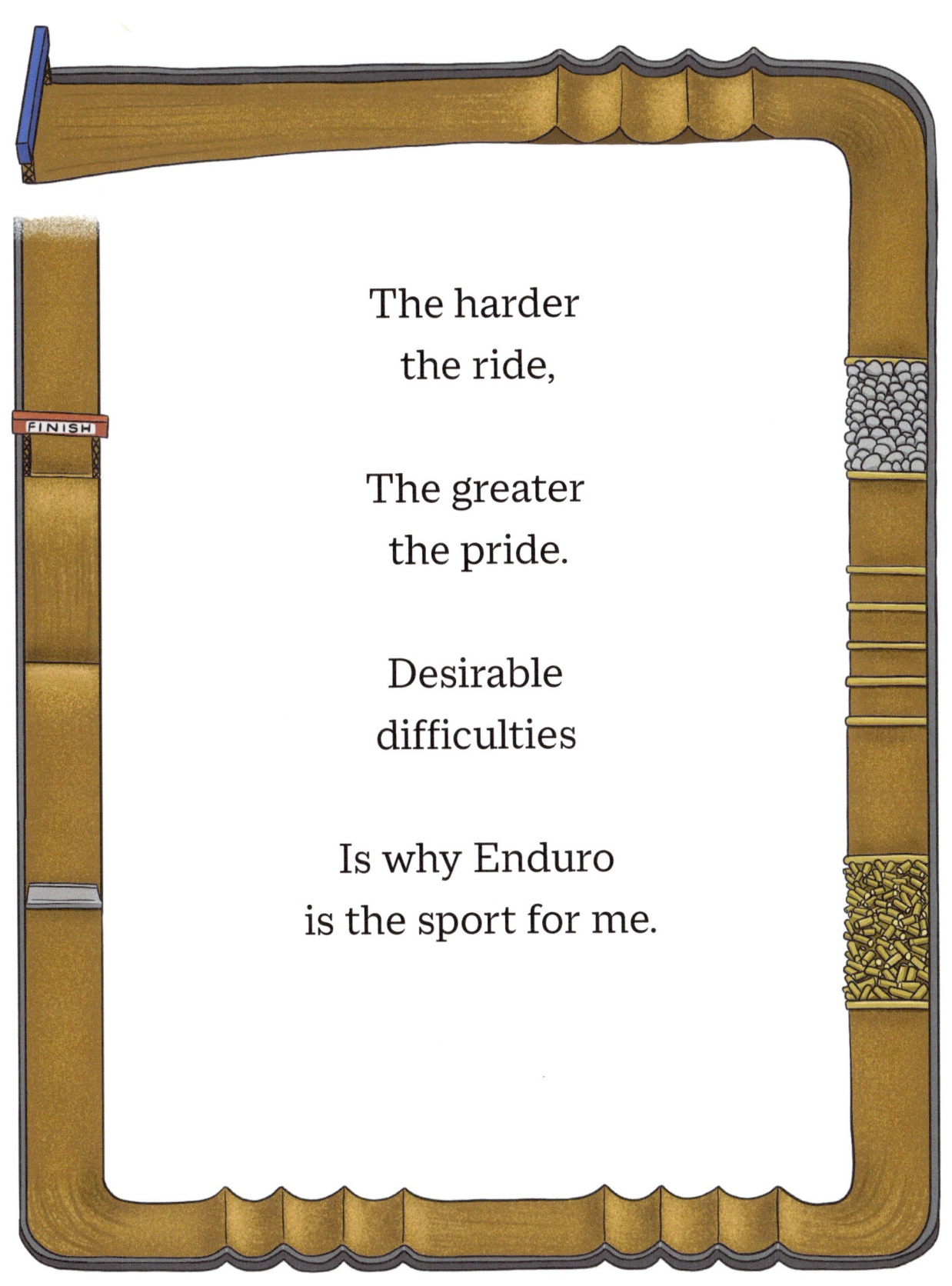

The harder
the ride,

The greater
the pride.

Desirable
difficulties

Is why Enduro
is the sport for me.

A Hare Scramble

Is no relaxing ramble

Risk versus reward, that's the gamble.

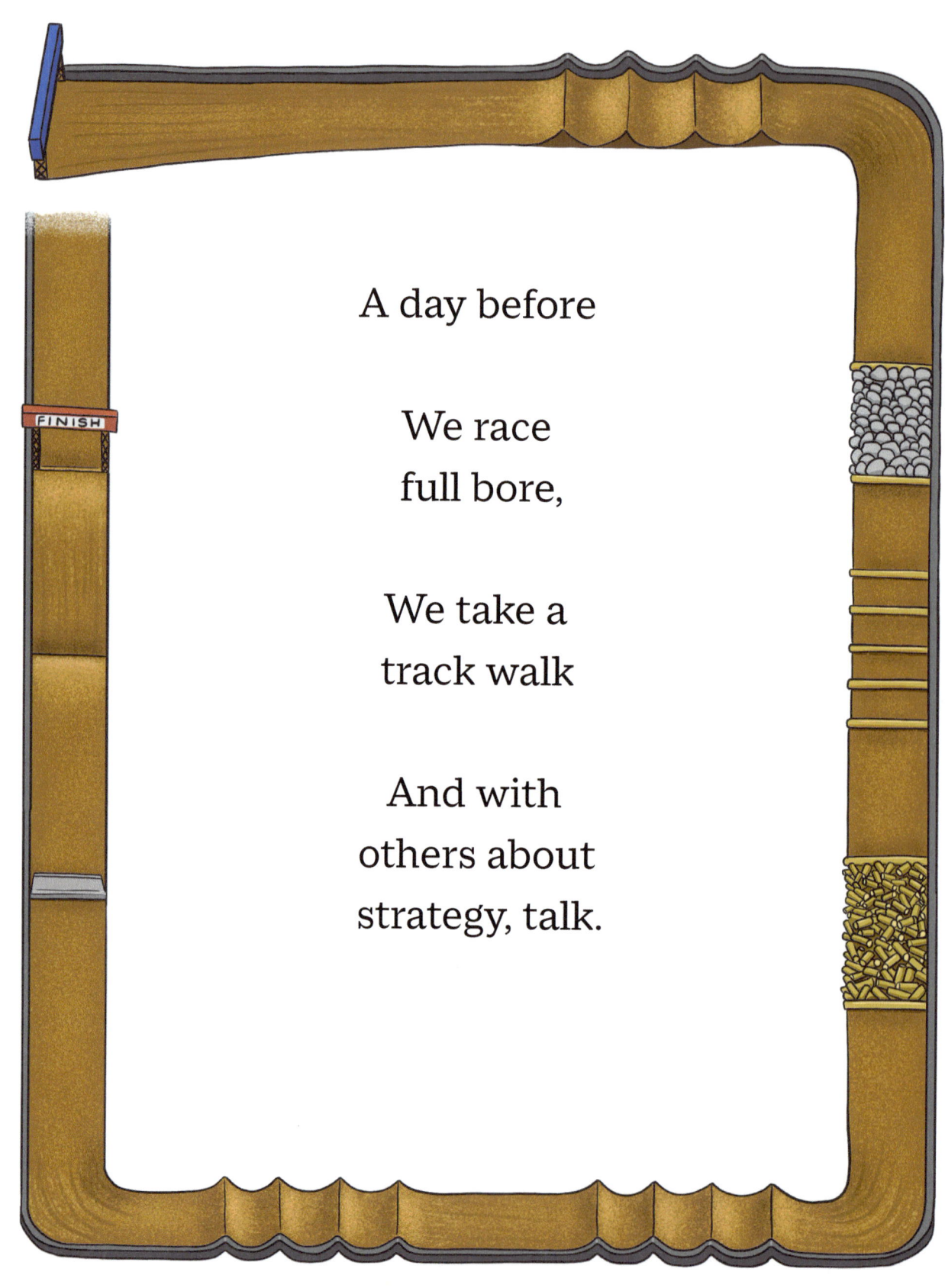

A day before

We race
full bore,

We take a
track walk

And with
others about
strategy, talk.

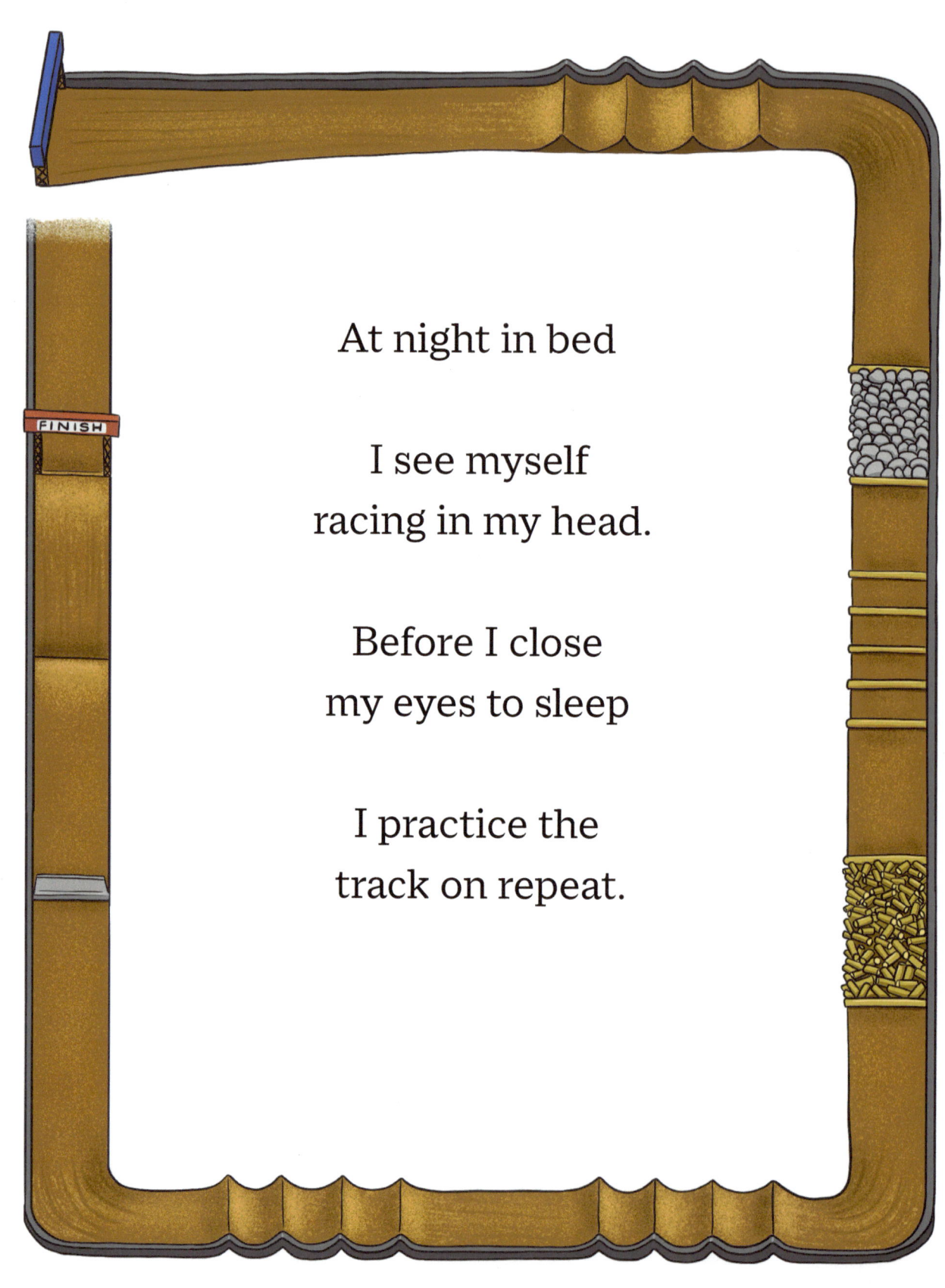

At night in bed

I see myself
racing in my head.

Before I close
my eyes to sleep

I practice the
track on repeat.

On race day

There's little left to say.

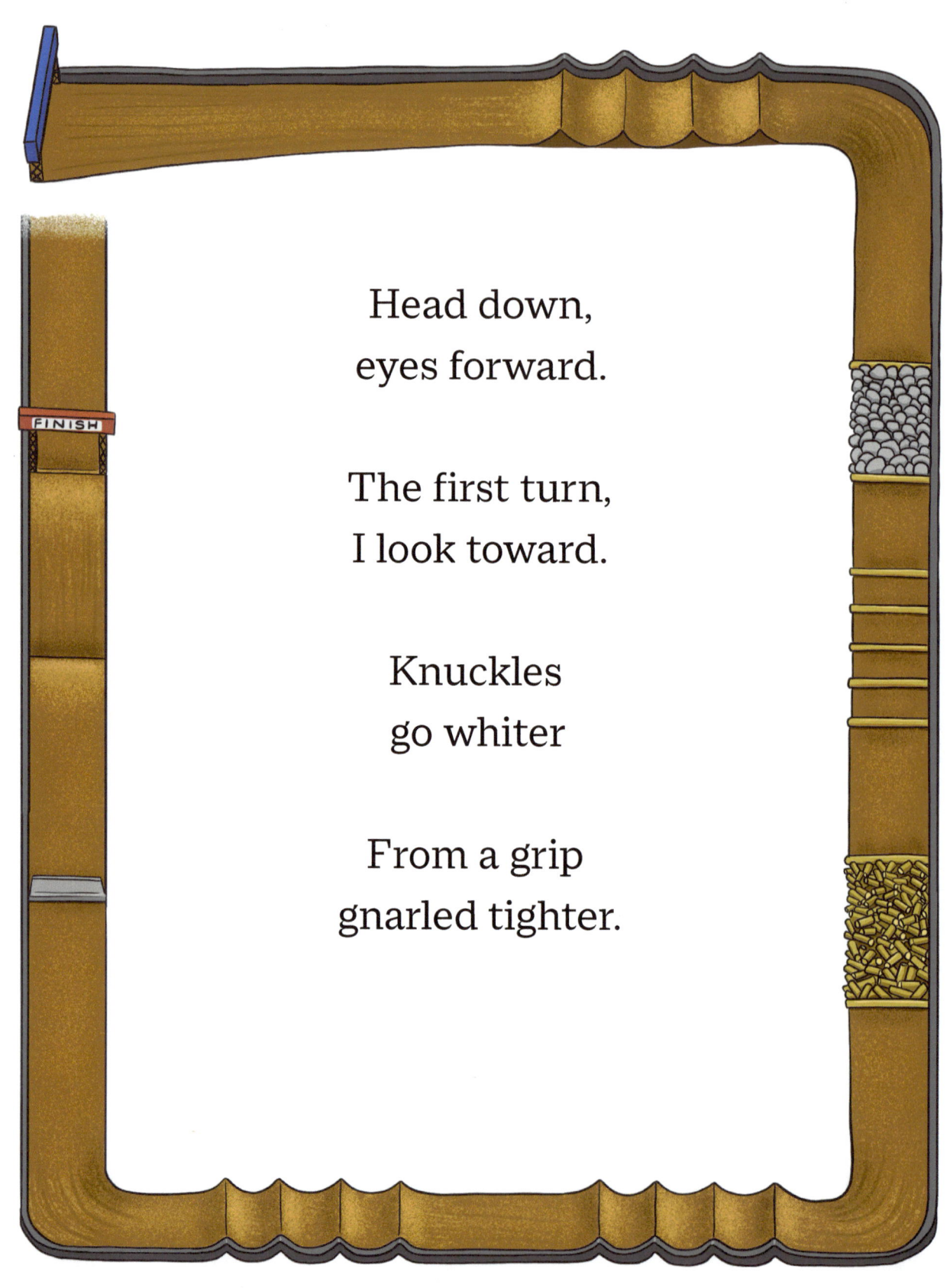

Head down,
eyes forward.

The first turn,
I look toward.

Knuckles
go whiter

From a grip
gnarled tighter.

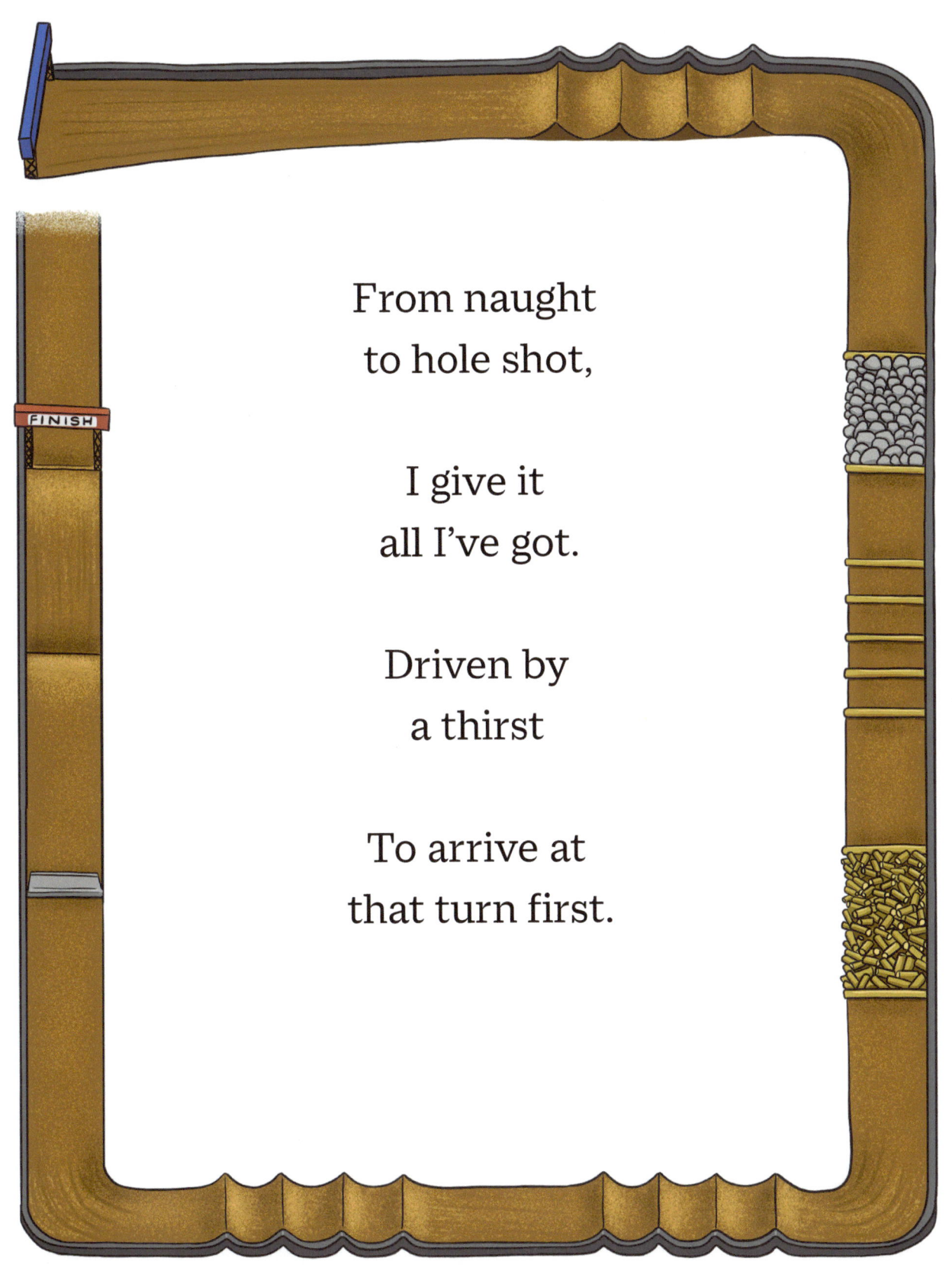

From naught
to hole shot,

I give it
all I've got.

Driven by
a thirst

To arrive at
that turn first.

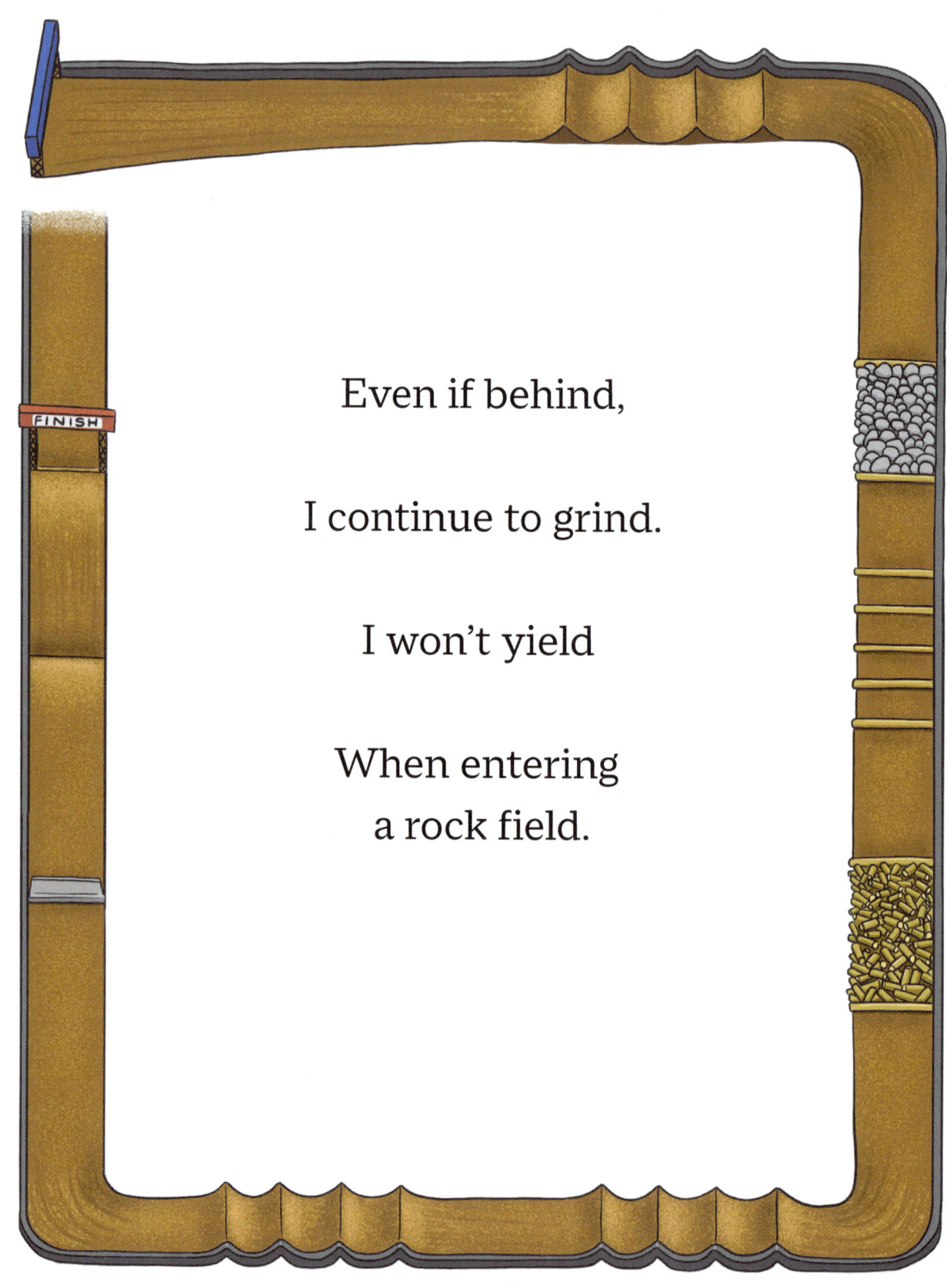

Even if behind,

I continue to grind.

I won't yield

When entering
a rock field.

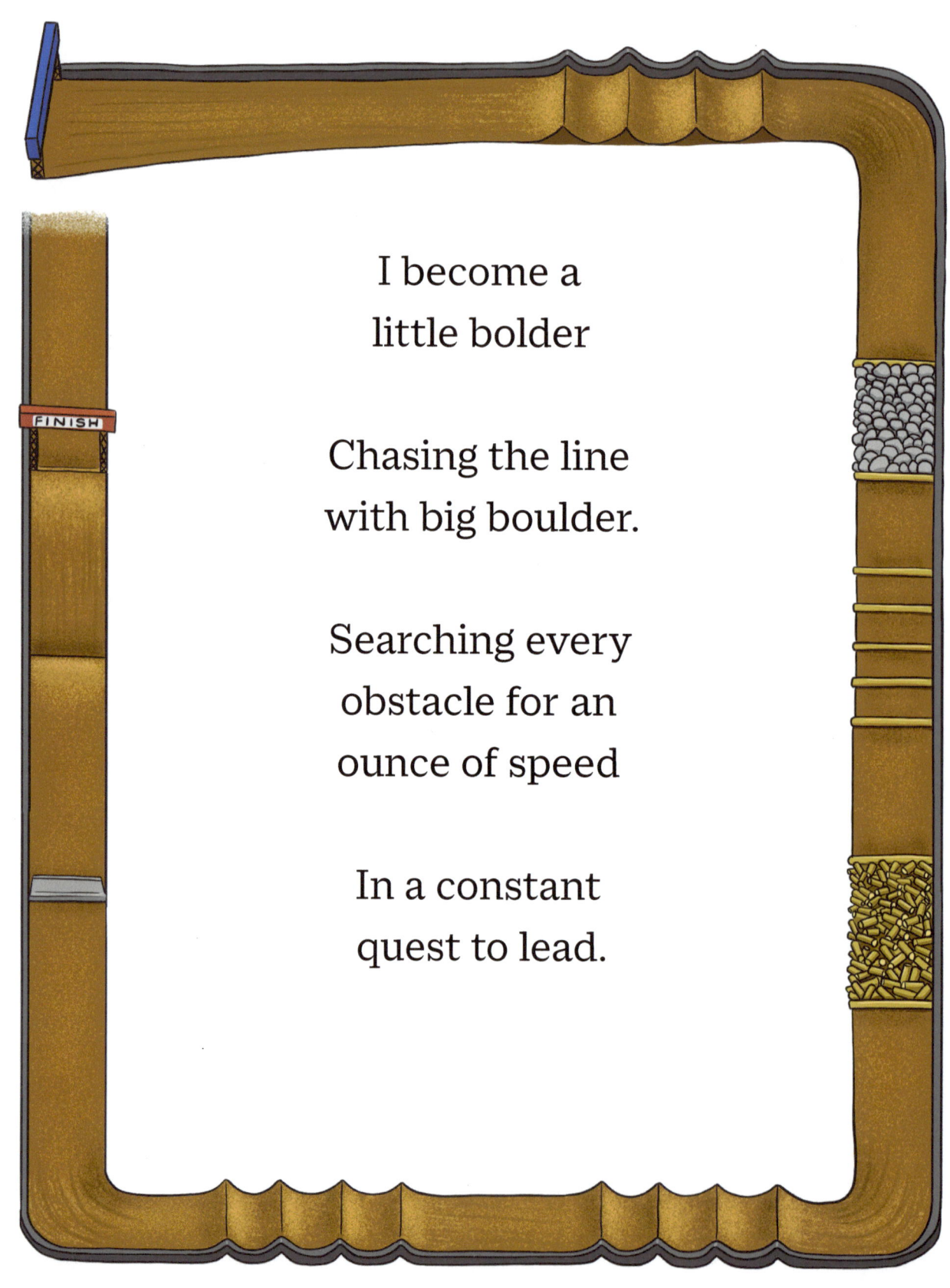

I become a little bolder

Chasing the line with big boulder.

Searching every obstacle for an ounce of speed

In a constant quest to lead.

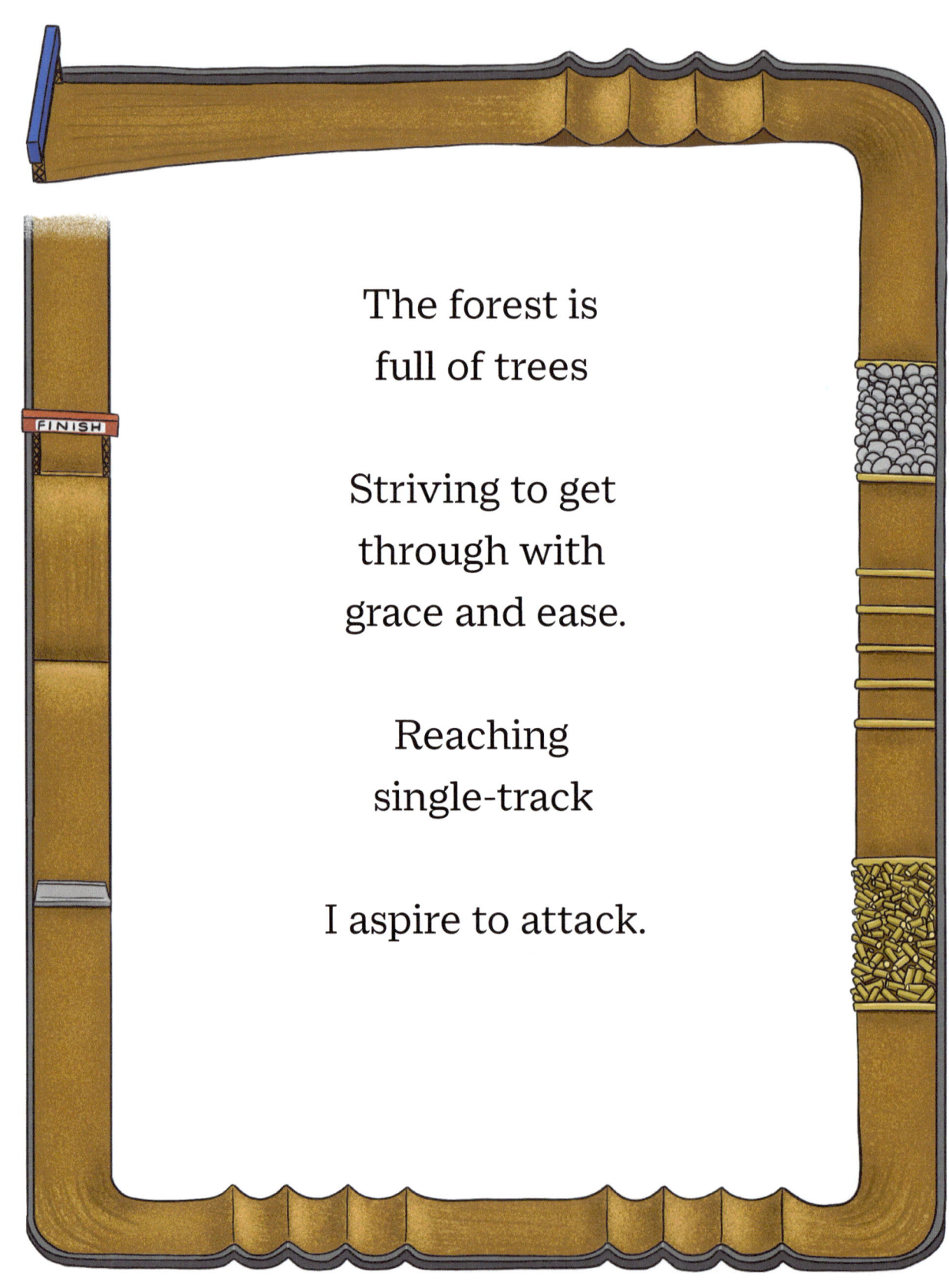

The forest is
full of trees

Striving to get
through with
grace and ease.

Reaching
single-track

I aspire to attack.

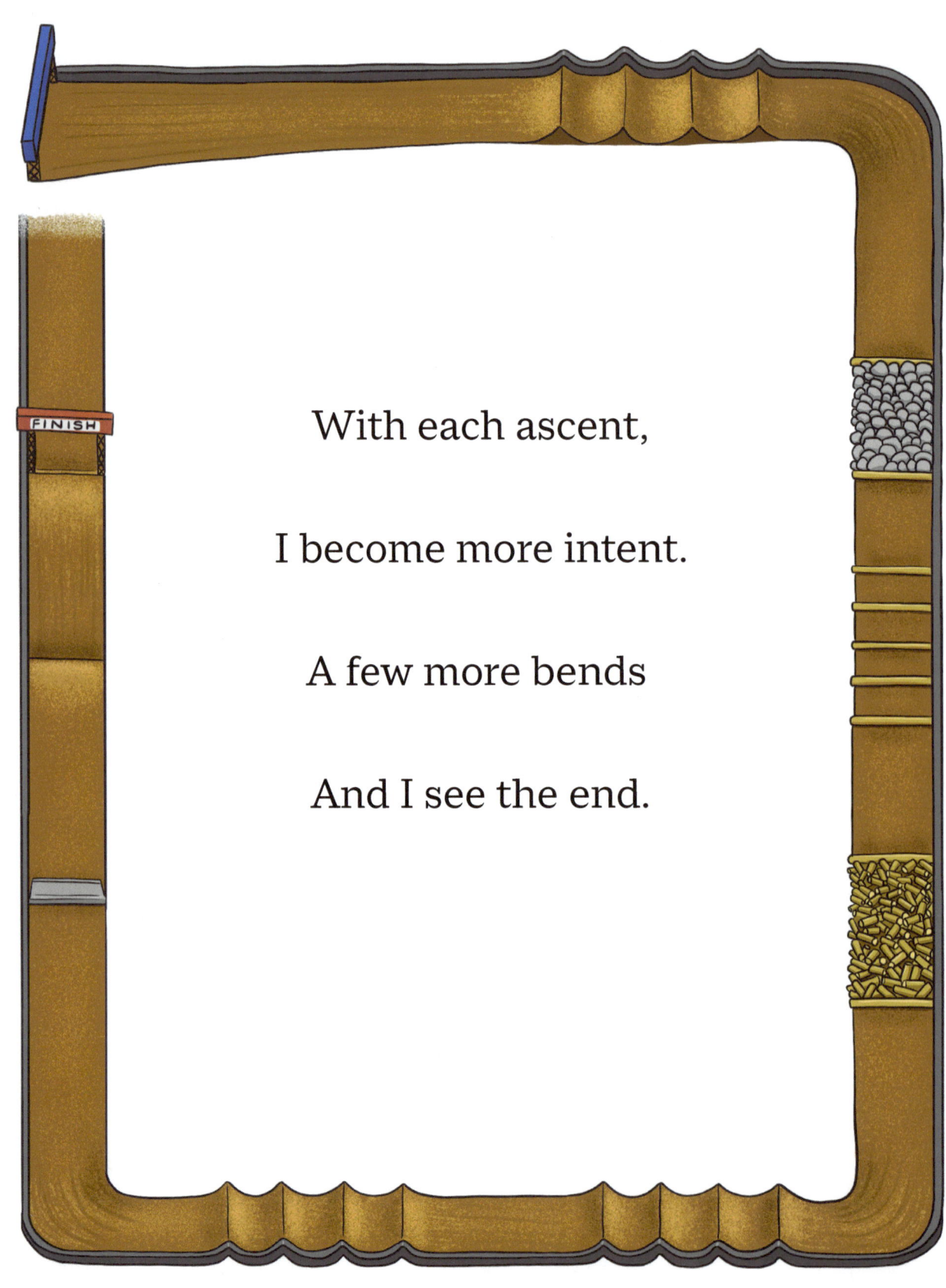

With each ascent,

I become more intent.

A few more bends

And I see the end.

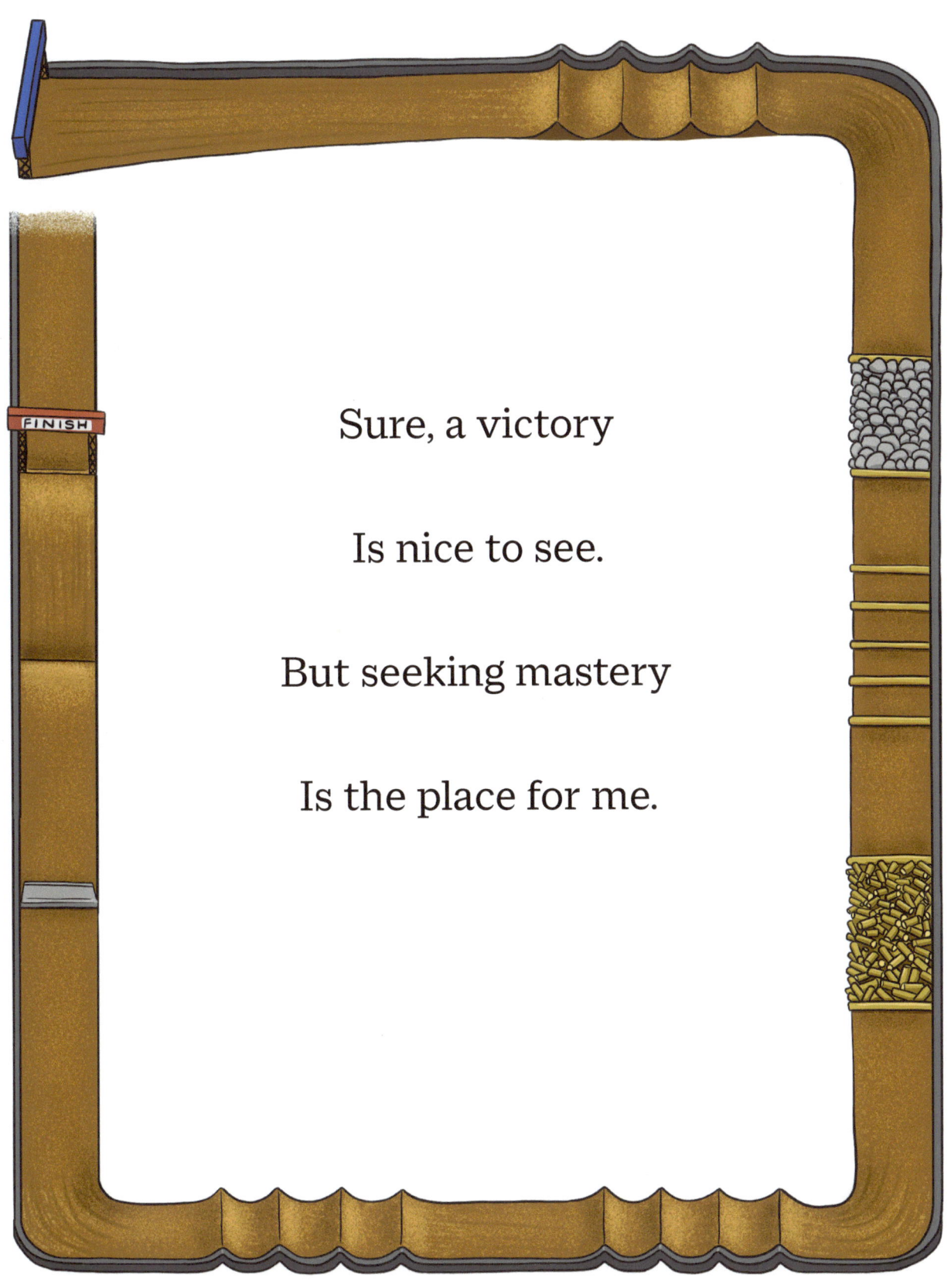

Sure, a victory

Is nice to see.

But seeking mastery

Is the place for me.

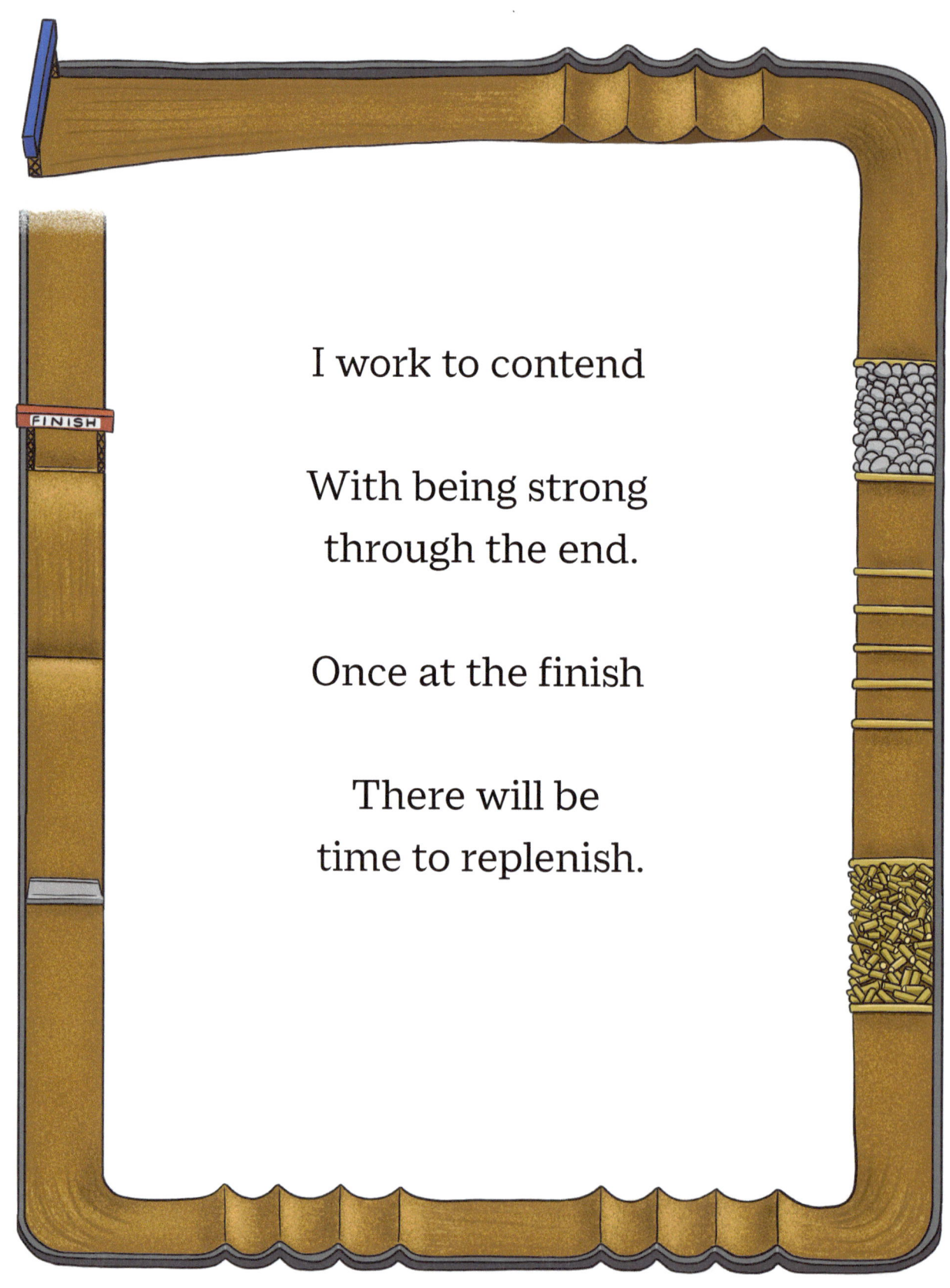

I work to contend

With being strong
through the end.

Once at the finish

There will be
time to replenish.

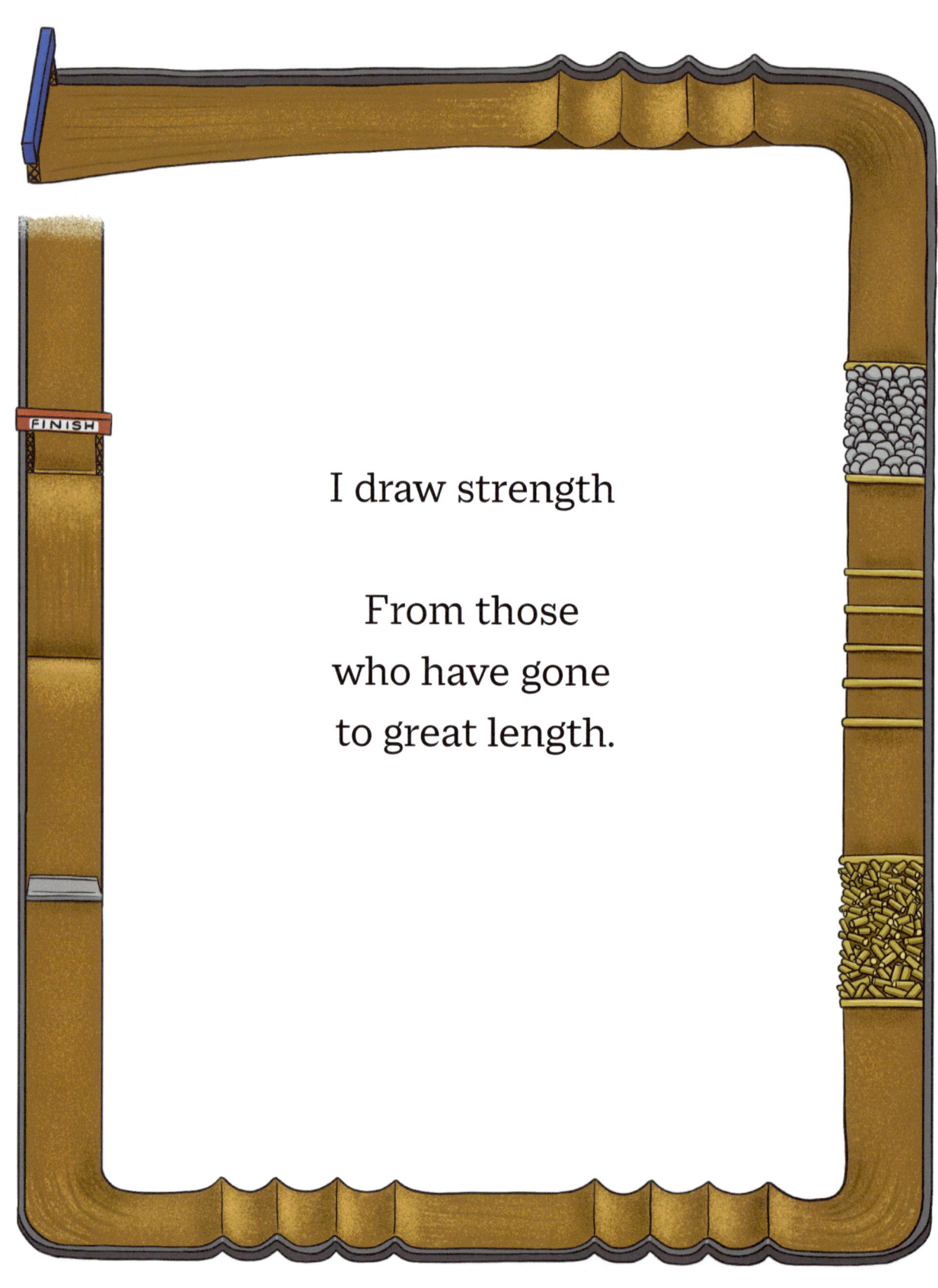

I draw strength

From those
who have gone
to great length.

Fans, friends, sponsors, and family.

All have helped me get right where I want to be.

www.ingramcontent.com/pod-product-compliance
Lightning Source LLC
Chambersburg PA
CBHW042247100526
44587CB00002B/54